CELEBRATING ALL PERSONALITIES

BY ABBY COLICH

BLUE OWL
BOOKS

TIPS FOR CAREGIVERS

Social and emotional learning (SEL) helps children manage emotions, learn how to feel empathy, create and achieve goals, and make good decisions. Strong lessons and support in SEL will help children establish positive habits in communication, cooperation, and decision-making. By incorporating SEL in early reading, children will learn the importance of accepting and celebrating all people in their communities.

BEFORE READING

Talk to the reader about personalities. Explain that personality has to do with how someone behaves and acts. Give examples of different personality traits.

Discuss: How would you describe your personality? How would you describe the personalities of your friends and family members? How are they similar or different?

AFTER READING

Talk to the reader about ways he or she can celebrate differences with others.

Discuss: What is one way you can accept another person's personality? Why should we accept others? Why is it good for a community to celebrate all people?

SEL GOAL

Children may have a loose understanding of acceptance and differences in personalities. Split the students into pairs, grouping students together who have seemingly different personalities. Prompt questions for them to ask one another. Talk to readers about the importance of empathy in accepting and celebrating the differences of others. Explain that our communities are better when everyone is accepted and included.

TABLE OF CONTENTS

CHAPTER 1

WHAT IS PERSONALITY?

Do people say you are friendly? Are you brave and curious? These are **traits**. Traits make up your **personality**. Personality is how someone thinks, feels, and **behaves**.

Your **community** is full of people with different personalities. Some people are outgoing. Others are quiet. Some people are serious. Others joke a lot. Different personalities can work well together to do great things.

Kyle's class is having a bake sale. Kyle is creative. He makes signs for the sale. Lana and Russ are active and hardworking. They bake the treats. Ava is **organized**. She talks with teachers. She figures out when and where to have the bake sale. Everyone works together to raise money for the class field trip!

MANY TRAITS

Every single person has many traits. You can be both funny and caring. Or maybe you are loyal and fair. Do you know what your traits are? If you're not sure, ask your close friends and family! Do you share any traits with these people?

CHAPTER 2

ACCEPT AND RESPECT

Do you and your best friend have similar personalities? It can be easy to get along with people who are like you. Maybe his or her personality is much different! Sometimes different personalities **complement** each other.

Sometimes it can take work to get along. Ben is very loud. Linn is very quiet. But they respect each other. This is what makes communities work! Plus, it feels good to **accept** others and to be accepted.

Having **empathy** helps us understand, accept, and respect others. Mel is nervous. Why? She has to give a speech in class. Emmy asks her how she feels. She listens to Mel. She thinks of a time she felt the same way. She tells Mel she understands.

WHAT TO SAY

Another way to show empathy is to **encourage** someone. Emmy tells Mel, "You can do it!" She reminds Mel how smart she is. She tells her that she can't wait to hear the speech. She is sure it will be great!

Even if you don't understand someone, show respect. Dax is very shy. Micah doesn't understand why he doesn't want to play soccer. But Micah doesn't make fun of Dax or get mad. Instead, he tells Dax he can play later if he wants to.

We can get along with others when we **compromise**. There is a group project at school. Everyone has different ideas. They listen to each other. Together, the group decides which idea to try first.

Get to know someone who is not like you. Find out what you have in common. You may find that you share some traits but not others. Or you may be more alike than you think. Others will see you being friendly. They may want to do the same.

GETTING ALONG

You don't have to be friends with everyone. Some people are very different from one another. But they can still respect and be kind to one another. What can you do to get along with people who aren't like you?

CHAPTER 3

BE YOU!

Be yourself! You have your own personality. Make a list of your traits. Are there any you want to add? Maybe your friend is always upbeat. You feel good when you are around her. You can work on being more upbeat, too!

Do you have traits you wish you could change? That's OK. People change as they grow up. Concentrate on what you like about yourself. When you accept yourself, it will help you accept others.

Everyone has his or her own personality. Each one is unique. When we learn to accept and respect others, we can work well with them. Then we can accomplish so much. What can your community do when people work together?

GOALS AND TOOLS

GROW WITH GOALS

Accepting all people, no matter their personality traits, is important. Focusing on people's positive qualities will help you be more accepting.

Goal: Name as many personality traits as you can. Can people have more than one? Why is it important to identify and understand personality traits?

Goal: Think of a time you showed empathy. If you can't think of anything, try to find a time when you can practice this. Do you see someone who is shy? Ask that person how he or she is feeling and why.

Goal: Get to know someone you haven't spoken with much before. Try to find one thing you have in common or that you both like.

WRITING REFLECTION

Accepting yourself can help you be more accepting of those around you.

1. What is one thing you like about yourself?

2. What is one thing about yourself that you wish you could change?

3. What is one thing you can do to be more accepting of others?

GLOSSARY

accept
To agree that something is correct, satisfactory, or enough.

behaves
Acts in a particular way.

community
A group of people who all have something in common.

complement
To complete or enhance something.

compromise
To agree to accept something that is not entirely what you wanted in order to satisfy some of the requests of other people.

empathy
The ability to understand and be sensitive to the thoughts and feelings of others.

encourage
To give someone confidence, usually by using praise and support.

organized
Prepared to run an event or activity or arrange the parts of something in a particular order or structure.

personality
All the qualities or traits that make one person different from others.

traits
Qualities or characteristics that make people different from each other.

TO LEARN MORE

FACT SURFER

Finding more information is as easy as 1, 2, 3.

1. Go to www.factsurfer.com

2. Enter "**celebratingallpersonalities**" into the search box.

3. Choose your cover to see a list of websites.

INDEX

Blue Owl Books are published by Jump!, 5357 Penn Avenue South, Minneapolis, MN 55419, www.jumplibrary.com

Copyright © 2021 Jump! International copyright reserved in all countries. No part of this book may be reproduced in any form without written permission from the publisher.

Library of Congress Cataloging-in-Publication Data

Names: Colich, Abby, author.
Title: Celebrating all personalities / Abby Colich.
Description: Minneapolis, MN: Jump!, [2021]
Series: Celebrating our communities | Blue Owl Books
Audience: Ages 7–10 | Audience: Grades 2–3
Identifiers: LCCN 2019050606 (print)
LCCN 2019050607 (ebook)
ISBN 9781645273714 (hardcover)
ISBN 9781645273721 (paperback)
ISBN 9781645273738 (ebook)
Subjects: LCSH: Personality–Juvenile literature. | Empathy–Juvenile literature.
Classification: LCC BF698 .C565 2021 (print) | LCC BF698 (ebook) | DDC 155.2/2–dc23
LC record available at https://lccn.loc.gov/2019050606
LC ebook record available at https://lccn.loc.gov/2019050607

Editor: Jenna Gleisner
Designer: Michelle Sonnek

Photo Credits: JohnnyGreig/iStock, cover (left); PeopleImages/iStock, cover (right); gradyreese/iStock, 1 (left); AJP/Shutterstock, 1 (right); In Green/Shutterstock, 3; martinedoucet/iStock, 4 (left); Gelpi/Shutterstock, 4 (right), 18; Inside Creative House/Shutterstock, 5; Monkey Business Images/Shutterstock, 6–7; Darrin Henry/Shutterstock, 8; FatCamera/iStock, 9; Motmotion Films/Shutterstock, 10–11; xujun/Shutterstock, 12–13 (background); Brocreative/Shutterstock, 12–13 (foreground); SDI Productions/iStock, 14–15; fstop123/iStock, 16–17; cheapbooks/Shutterstock, 19; Tetra Images, LLC/Alamy, 20–21.

Printed in the United States of America at Corporate Graphics in North Mankato, Minnesota.